Pebble Plus

LET'S LOOK AT COUNTRIES

LET'S LOOK AT

SOUTH AFRICA

BY NIKKI BRUNO CLAPPER

CAPSTONE PRESS
a capstone imprint

Pebble Plus is published by Capstone Press,
1710 Roe Crest Drive, North Mankato, Minnesota 56003
www.mycapstone.com

Library of Congress Cataloging-in-Publication Data
Names: Clapper, Nikki Bruno, author.
Title: Let's look at South Africa / by Nikki Bruno Clapper.
Description: North Mankato, Minnesota : Capstone Press, [2018] | Series:
  Pebble plus. Let's look at countries | Includes bibliographical references
  and index. | Audience: Ages 4-8.
Identifiers: LCCN 2017037877 (print) | LCCN 2017038536 (ebook) | ISBN
  9781515799283 (eBook PDF) | ISBN 9781515799160 (hardcover) | ISBN
  9781515799221 (pbk.)
Subjects: LCSH: South Africa--Juvenile literature.
Classification: LCC DT1719 (ebook) | LCC DT1719 .C55 2018 2018 (print) | DDC
  968--dc23
LC record available at https://lccn.loc.gov/2017037877

Editorial Credits
Juliette Peters, designer; Tracy Cummins, media researcher; Laura Manthe, production specialist

Photo Credits
Getty Images: Francois Nel, 16; iStockphoto: Henrique NDR Martins, 13, ManoAfrica, 1;
Shutterstock: Andrea Willmore, 22-23, 24, bonchan, 19, Denis Mironov, 21, elleon, 9, Francesco
Dazzi, 5, Garth Fuchs, Cover Top, Globe Turner, 22 Top, Hedrus, 11, JMx Images, 10, Linda
Nienaber, Cover Bottom, Cover Back, Mai Groves, 17, Monkey Business Images, 15, nale, 4, Olaf
Holland, 3, Richard van der Spuy, 6-7, Utopia_88, Cover Middle

Note to Parents and Teachers

The Let's Look at Countries set supports national curriculum standards for social studies related to
people, places, and culture. This book describes and illustrates South Africa. The images support
early readers in understanding the text. The repetition of words and phrases helps early readers
learn new words. This book also introduces early readers to subject-specific vocabulary words,
which are defined in the Glossary section. Early readers may need assistance to read some words
and to use the Table of Contents, Glossary, Read More, Internet Sites, Critical Thinking Questions,
and Index sections of the book.

Printed in the United States of America.
1906

TABLE OF CONTENTS

Where Is South Africa?

South Africa is a country
at the southern tip of Africa.
Its capitals are Pretoria,
Cape Town, and Bloemfontein.

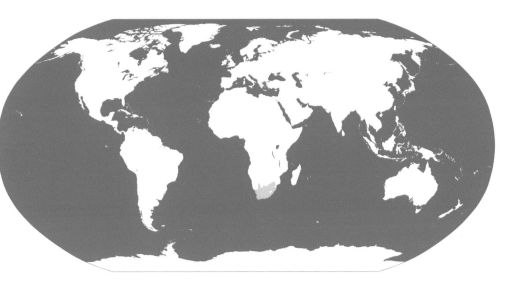

South Africa

From Grasslands to Mountains

Much of South Africa's land is a plateau covered in grasslands. The climate is dry. Droughts are common.

Mountain ranges surround

the grasslands in a U shape.

The most famous range

is called the Drakensberg.

This means "Dragon's Mountain."

In the Wild

Leopards, cheetahs, and lions live in the grasslands. They hunt zebras, wildebeest, and antelope. Penguins live along the coast.

lion

zebras

People

South Africa's people have many different backgrounds. Most people are black. Others are white, Asian, or mixed race.

On the Job

Some South Africans

work in gold mines.

Others build cars or

make clothes in factories.

Tourism jobs are common.

On the Field

Many South Africans love sports. Rugby, boxing, and running are popular. Athletes climb, bike, and hike in the mountains.

rugby

At the Table

South Africans eat a lot of meat. The meat is often barbecued or dried. Bobotie has baked meat mixed with egg and fruit.

bobotie

Famous Site

Table Mountain towers

over the city of Cape Town.

The mountain has a flat top.

People climb it on foot or

in a cable car.

QUICK SOUTH AFRICA FACTS

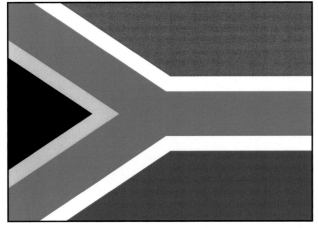
South African flag

Name: Republic of South Africa

Capitals: Pretoria, Cape Town, Bloemfontein

Other major cities: Johannesburg, Durban

Population: 54,300,704 (July 2016 estimate)

Size: 470,693 square miles (1,219,090 sq km)

Languages: isiZulu, isiXhosa, Afrikaans, English, isiNdebele, SeSotho, Sesotho sa Leboa, SiSwati, Xitsonga, Setswana, Tshivenda

Money: rand

GLOSSARY

background—information that helps describe a person, such as race, education level, and religion

cable car—a car pulled by an overhead or underground cable

capital—the city in a country where the government is based

climate—average weather of a place throughout the year

drought—when the land is dry because of too little rain

mine—a place where workers dig up minerals that are underground

plateau—an area of high, flat land

tourism—the business of taking care of visitors to a country or place

READ MORE

Aloian, Molly. *Cultural Traditions in South Africa.* Cultural Traditions in My World. New York: Crabtree Publishing Company, 2014.

Perkins, Chloe. *Living in . . . South Africa.* Living in . . . New York: Simon Spotlight, 2016.

Shoup, Kate. *South Africa.* New York: Cavendish Square Publishing, 2018.

INTERNET SITES

Use FactHound to find Internet sites related to this book.

Visit *www.facthound.com*

Just type 9781515799160 and go.

Check out projects, games and lots more at
www.capstonekids.com

CRITICAL THINKING QUESTIONS

1. What are some sports and activities South Africans enjoy?

2. What is a capital?

3. How can people get to the top of Table Mountain?

INDEX

5